BEST PYTHON PROGRAMMING BOOK

"From Novice to Python Pro:

Elevate Your Skills with

Step-by-Step Mastery and Insider

Secrets for Career Success!"

Richard M. Butler

Table of Contents

Part 1: Building Your Python Foundation

This is where your Python adventure begins! We'll establish a strong foundation by equipping you with the essential building blocks that form the core of your Python mastery. You'll delve into the world of Python, explore its applications, and set up your development environment.

We'll then embark on a journey to master the basics. Unveil the fundamental building blocks of Python programs, including variables and different data types (numbers, text, etc.). Learn how to manipulate these elements using operators to perform calculations and create dynamic programs.

Finally, you'll gain control of your programs! We'll explore how to make decisions using conditional statements and automate repetitive tasks with loops.

By the end of Part 1, you'll have a solid understanding of Python's syntax, data structures, and control flow mechanisms, laying the groundwork for more advanced concepts.

Chapter 1: Introduction to Python Programming

Welcome to the thrilling world of Python programming! This chapter serves as your gateway, where you'll:

- **Discover the Power of Python:** We'll explore the vast applications of Python, from web development and data analysis to automation and machine learning. You'll understand why Python is considered such a versatile and in-demand language.

- **Unveil the Python Landscape:** Get a glimpse of the development environment you'll be using to write and run your Python code. We'll walk you through the installation process and introduce you to the basic tools you'll need.

- **Take Your First Steps:** Dive into some simple

   Python code examples to get a feel for the

   language's syntax and structure.

   You'll learn how to write basic commands and

   see the results instantly.

By the end of this chapter, you'll be equipped with a

foundational understanding of what Python is and how it

works. You'll be excited to move on to Part 2 and delve

deeper into the core elements of Python programming!

Chapter 2: Mastering the Basics: Variables, Data Types & Operators

This chapter equips you with the building blocks of any Python program: variables, data types, and operators. Buckle up as we embark on a journey to understand:

- **Variables**: Imagine little boxes that store information you can use throughout your program. We'll explore how to create variables with meaningful names and understand the rules for using them effectively.

- **Data Types:** Not all information is created equal! Learn about the different data types Python offers, like numbers (integers, floats), text (strings), and logical values (booleans).

  We'll delve into how to assign specific data types to your variables and explore the operations you can perform on each type.

- **Operators:** These are the tools that allow you to manipulate your data! We'll cover arithmetic operators for calculations (addition, subtraction, etc.), comparison operators for making decisions (greater than, less than, etc.), and even assignment operators for storing values in your variables.

Chapter 3: Control Flow: Making Decisions and Looping

Ever wished your program could think for itself? Well, in Python, you can achieve a similar effect using control flow! This chapter equips you with two essential tools: conditional statements and loops, allowing your programs to make decisions and repeat tasks automatically.

Taking the Reins with Conditional Statements:

Imagine your program encountering a situation – is a user's age greater than 18? Is a certain file present? Conditional statements, specifically if and else, let your program respond accordingly. We'll explore:

- The if statement: This acts like a question your program asks. Based on the answer (True or

False), the program executes a specific block of code.

- The else statement: This provides an alternative course of action if the condition in the if statement is False.

By mastering these statements, you'll empower your programs to react differently depending on the circumstances, making them more versatile and user-friendly.

Automating Repetitive Tasks with Loops:

Sometimes, you might need your program to perform the same action multiple times. Loops come to the rescue! We'll delve into two powerful loop constructs:

- The for loop: This is ideal when you know exactly how many times you want to repeat a task. It provides a clean and concise way to iterate over a sequence of items, like a list of numbers or names.
- The while loop: This loop keeps repeating a block of code as long as a certain condition remains True. It's perfect for situations where you don't know the exact number of repetitions beforehand.

By the time this chapter ends, you will know how to::

- Craft programs that make informed decisions based on conditions.
- Automate repetitive tasks using for and while loops, saving you time and effort.

- Combine conditional statements and loops to create more powerful and dynamic programs.

Mastering control flow unlocks a new level of possibilities in your Python programming journey. Get ready to build interactive programs that can react to situations and automate repetitive tasks, making your code more efficient and intelligent!

Part 2: Working with Python Power Tools

You've conquered the basics, now it's time to unlock Python's true potential! This section equips you with essential tools to streamline your coding experience and build more powerful applications.

Get ready to explore ways to organise your data efficiently using lists, tuples, and dictionaries. Imagine these as specialised containers, each with its strengths, to keep your code clean and organised.

We'll also delve into the concept of functions, the building blocks of reusable code. Master the art of defining functions, providing them with data (arguments), and capturing their results (return values).

This empowers you to write concise, modular code that saves time and promotes better organisation.

By the end of Part 2, you'll be wielding powerful tools to structure your data effectively and write reusable, efficient code. This sets the stage for building more sophisticated applications in the chapters to come!

Chapter 4: Lists, Tuples, and Dictionaries: Organising Your Data Like a Pro

Imagine a workbench overflowing with tools – it would be a nightmare to find anything! Python offers similar functionality, but for data, with lists, tuples, and dictionaries. These powerful structures will help you organise your information efficiently, making your code more readable and manageable.

- **Lists:** Think of a grocery list – items in a specific order. Lists are flexible collections of items, perfect for storing ordered sequences of data. You can add, remove, and rearrange elements within a list, making them ideal for dynamic data sets.
- **Tuples**: Similar to lists, but with a twist – tuples are immutable, meaning their contents cannot be changed once created.

  Think of a historical record – the information shouldn't be modified. Tuples offer a secure way to store data that shouldn't be altered.

- **Dictionaries:** Ever wished you could find information based on nicknames? Dictionaries excel at this! They store data as key-value pairs, allowing you to retrieve information quickly using unique keys. Imagine a phonebook – you look up a name (key) to find the phone number (value).

By the end of this chapter, you'll be a master of data organisation! You'll be able to:

- Choose the right data structure (list, tuple, or dictionary) based on your needs.
- Create, modify, and access elements within these structures.
- Leverage the power of dictionaries for efficient key-based data retrieval.

This newfound ability to organise your data effectively will be a game-changer in your Python programming journey. Get ready to write cleaner, more maintainable code as you embark on building more complex applications in the following chapters!

Chapter 5: Functions: Building Reusable Blocks of Code

Ever feel like you're rewriting the same code over and over again? Well, fret no more! This chapter introduces functions, the superheroes of Python programming that promote code reusability and efficiency.

Imagine a toolbox filled with specialised tools for different tasks. Functions act similarly, encapsulating specific functionalities into self-contained blocks of code. Here's what you'll learn:

- Defining Functions: We'll explore how to create functions, giving them meaningful names and defining the specific actions they'll perform. Think of it as designing a tool – you specify its purpose and functionality.

- The Power of Arguments: Functions are rarely loners! They can accept data, called arguments, which they can use to operate on. Imagine providing a wrench with the nut size (argument) to perform its job effectively.

- Returning Values: Just like a tool might return a finished product, functions can return values after completing their tasks. This allows you to capture the results of a function's execution and use them elsewhere in your program.

By mastering functions, you'll be able to:

- Write concise and reusable code: Avoid code duplication by creating functions that can be used multiple times throughout your program.
- Improve code readability and maintainability: Functions break down complex problems into smaller, more manageable chunks, making your code easier to understand and modify.
- Promote modular programming: Functions encourage a modular approach, where different parts of your program are independent and well-defined.

This newfound ability to build reusable code is a cornerstone of efficient Python programming. Get ready to write cleaner, more maintainable code as you embark on building more complex applications in the following chapters!

Part 3: Level Up Your Python Skills

Now that you've mastered the fundamentals and harnessed Python's power tools, it's time to elevate your skills and explore advanced concepts. This section will equip you to:

- **Work with External Data and Errors**: Learn how to interact with files on your computer, allowing you to store and retrieve data persistently. We'll also delve into exception handling, a technique for gracefully managing errors that might occur during program execution.

- **Embrace Object-Oriented Programming:** Discover a powerful programming paradigm that revolves around objects and their interactions. This will empower you to create more robust and maintainable code.

By the end of Part 3, you'll be equipped to tackle more complex problems and unlock the full potential of Python in various real-world applications.

Chapter 6: Files and Exception Handling: Working with External Data and Errors

In this chapter, you'll venture beyond the confines of your program's memory and explore two crucial aspects of working with Python:

- **Files and External Data:** Imagine your program needing to store information beyond its current execution. Files come to the rescue! We'll delve into:
    - Reading from Files: Learn how to open and access data stored in external files on your computer.
    - Writing to Files: Discover how to create new files and store data persistently for future use.

- **Exception Handling:** Even the best-written programs can encounter errors during execution. Exception handling equips you to gracefully manage these errors, preventing your program from crashing unexpectedly. We'll explore:
  - Identifying Exceptions: Learn how to recognize potential errors (exceptions) that might occur in your code.
  - Handling Exceptions: Discover techniques for catching these exceptions and providing meaningful responses, ensuring your program continues to run smoothly even when errors arise.

Once you understand these ideas, you'll be able to ;

- Persistently store and retrieve data, allowing your programs to work with information beyond their current execution.

- Write robust and user-friendly code that can handle unexpected errors gracefully.

- Develop more sophisticated applications that interact with external data sources.

This newfound ability to work with files and handle errors is a critical step towards building professional-grade Python applications!

Chapter 7: Object-Oriented Programming: Creating Powerful Structures

Get ready to unlock a whole new way of thinking about programs! This chapter introduces Object-Oriented Programming (OOP), a powerful paradigm that will transform how you approach building complex applications in Python.

Imagine a blueprint for a house – it defines the structure, components, and how they interact. OOP is similar, but for software development. It revolves around creating objects, which are like self-contained entities that encapsulate data (attributes) and the actions they can perform (methods).

Here's what you'll delve into:

- **Understanding Objects and Classes:** We'll explore the concept of classes, which act as blueprints for creating objects. A class defines the attributes and methods that all objects of that type will share. Think of the class as the house blueprint, and each object as a unique house built from that plan.

- **Building with Classes and Objects**: Learn how to define classes in Python, specifying the attributes and methods objects of that class will possess. We'll also explore how to create objects (instances) from these classes and utilise their functionalities.

- **Relationships Between Objects:** The beauty of OOP lies in how objects can interact with each other.

  We'll explore concepts like inheritance (creating specialised objects from existing ones) and polymorphism (objects responding differently to the same message), allowing you to build more modular and reusable code.

By mastering OOP, you'll be able to:

- **Organise complex code:** Break down your program into well-defined objects, making your code more maintainable and easier to understand.
- **Promote code reusability:** Leverage inheritance to create specialised objects from existing ones, saving you time and effort.

- **Model real-world entities:** Think of objects as real-world things (cars, customers, etc.) with properties and behaviours, making your code more intuitive and easier to reason about.

This newfound ability to leverage OOP principles will empower you to build more sophisticated and robust Python applications in the chapters to come!

Part 4: Unveiling Python Secrets for Professionals

This section equips you with the knowledge and tools used by professional Python developers. Get ready to:

- Explore Python's vast ecosystem of libraries and frameworks. These pre-written collections of code provide powerful functionalities for various tasks, saving you time and effort.
- Delve into building real-world projects. Put your newfound skills to the test by creating practical Python applications that address real-world problems.

By the end of Part 4, you'll have a solid understanding of how professional developers leverage Python's capabilities and be well on your way to building impressive projects and potentially landing your dream Python developer job.

Chapter 8: Advanced Libraries and Frameworks: Exploring Python's Ecosystem

The Python landscape extends far beyond the core language! This chapter unveils Python's rich ecosystem of libraries and frameworks, powerful tools used by professional developers to streamline their workflow and achieve complex tasks efficiently.

Imagine a toolbox overflowing with specialised tools – that's the essence of Python's libraries and frameworks. They offer pre-written code for various functionalities, saving you time and effort when tackling specific problems. Here's what you'll explore:

- **A World of Libraries:** We'll delve into popular libraries like NumPy for scientific computing, pandas for data analysis, and Matplotlib for data visualisation. You'll discover how these libraries streamline tasks in their respective domains.

- **The Power of Frameworks:** Frameworks provide a more comprehensive structure for building complex applications. We'll explore frameworks like Django for web development and TensorFlow for machine learning. You'll understand how these frameworks offer a foundation and essential tools to accelerate your development process.

By the end of this chapter, you'll be equipped to:

- **Identify the right tools for the job:** Gain a solid understanding of the various libraries and frameworks available within the Python ecosystem.

- **Leverage pre-written code:** Learn how to utilise libraries and frameworks to achieve complex functionalities without reinventing the wheel.

- **Become a more efficient developer:** Discover how these tools can streamline your development process, allowing you to focus on the unique aspects of your project.

This newfound knowledge of Python's vast ecosystem empowers you to approach real-world problems with confidence and efficiency. Get ready to explore building your own projects in the next chapter!

Chapter 9: Building Real-World Projects: Putting Your Skills to Action

It's time to showcase your Python prowess! This chapter guides you through the exciting process of building real-world projects, putting your newly acquired skills into practice.

Imagine transforming your theoretical knowledge into tangible applications that solve problems or automate tasks. Here's what you'll delve into:

- **Identifying Project Ideas:** We'll explore strategies for brainstorming and selecting project ideas that align with your interests and challenge your skillset.
- **Planning and Design:** Learn how to break down your project into manageable phases, defining clear goals and designing the overall structure.

- **Building and Testing:** Get ready to code! We'll walk you through the process of implementing your project step-by-step, utilising the libraries and techniques you've learned throughout this book. Testing is crucial, so we'll explore strategies to ensure your project functions as intended.

- **Deployment (Optional):** Consider how you might share your creation with the world! We'll touch upon concepts like deploying your project as a web application or creating an executable file for others to use.

By the end of this chapter, you'll have not only a functional Python project but also a deeper understanding of the entire development lifecycle. This experience will boost your confidence, showcase your skills to potential employers, and solidify your journey as a Python developer.

Part 5: Your Journey to Python Proficiency

The final leg of your Python adventure equips you with the tools and knowledge to excel as a Python developer. Get ready to:

- Master debugging techniques, transforming you into a problem-solving ninja!
- Explore exciting career paths within the vast world of Python development.
- Learn strategies to land your dream Python developer job and embark on a fulfilling career.

By the end of Part 5, you'll be a confident and well-rounded Python developer, ready to tackle real-world challenges and make your mark in the ever-evolving world of technology.

Chapter 10: Debugging Techniques: Troubleshooting Your Code Like a Pro

Even the most seasoned programmers encounter errors (bugs) in their code. This chapter equips you with essential debugging techniques, transforming you from a frustrated beginner to a problem-solving ninja!

Imagine your program acting strangely – unexpected results or crashes can be a nightmare. But fear not! Here's your debugging toolkit:

- **Understanding Errors:** We'll explore different types of errors you might encounter, from syntax errors (typos) to runtime errors (issues that arise during program execution). Learning to identify the error type is the first step towards fixing it.

- **The Art of Printing:** Sometimes, a simple print statement can be your best friend. We'll delve into strategic use of print statements to inspect the values of variables at different points in your code, helping you pinpoint where things go wrong.

- **Leveraging Debuggers:** Python provides a built-in debugger called pdb. We'll explore how to use pdb to step through your code line by line, examine variable values, and set breakpoints to pause execution at specific points. This allows you to analyse your code's behaviour in real-time.

- **Logical Reasoning and Code Review:** Debugging isn't just about fancy tools. We'll explore strategies for applying logical reasoning and code review techniques to identify and fix errors.Sometimes an outside viewpoint or a new set of eyes can do wonders.

Gaining proficiency with these debugging methods will enable you to : Efficiently identify and fix errors in your code, saving you time and frustration.

- Develop a systematic approach to problem-solving, making you a more confident and resourceful programmer.
- Write cleaner and more reliable code by proactively identifying potential issues before they arise.

Chapter 11: Career Paths with Python: Exploring Opportunities and Landing Your Dream Job

Congratulations! You've conquered the fundamentals of Python and are well on your way to becoming a skilled developer. This chapter sets your sights on the exciting world of Python careers. We'll explore:

- The Diverse Landscape of Python Development: Python's versatility opens doors to various career paths. We'll delve into popular areas like web development, data science, machine learning, automation scripting, and scientific computing. Discover how your interests and skills can align with these exciting opportunities.

- Building Your Developer Portfolio: Showcase your Python prowess! We'll explore strategies for building a compelling developer portfolio that highlights your projects, skills, and problem-solving abilities. This portfolio serves as a powerful tool to impress potential employers.

- The Art of the Job Search: Learn effective strategies for crafting a winning resume and cover letter that tailor your Python skills to specific job requirements. We'll also explore resources for finding Python development jobs and acing job interviews.

By the end of this chapter, you'll be equipped with a roadmap to navigate the exciting world of Python careers. You'll have a clear understanding of potential paths, a captivating portfolio to showcase your skills, and the knowledge to confidently land your dream job as a Python developer.